# Dating a Narcissist

*How to Kill a Narcissist at the Very First Date. Set Boundaries to Avoid a Nightmare and Becoming Psychopath free . Dating after the Narcissistic Abuse. Recovery and Healing*

Author

*Dana Jackson & Ross Covert*

# Table of Contents

# Introduction

Congratulations on your purchase of *Dating a Narcissist,* and thank you for investing in it. Inside you will find all the information you need to understand if you have started dating a narcissist and the tactics they will use to try and lure you into their web of chaos.

There are specific tricks that the narcissist uses to draw even the most intelligent people to them. Knowing what to look for can help protect you from the abuse that starts to happen once they have you in their grips. From the way they present themselves to the manipulation and lies, narcissists will go to great lengths to pull the wool over your eyes and get you to play their game.

We are going to look over the narcissist's favorite tools that help bring people down. These are things like love bombing, gaslighting, and devaluation. There are many more, and we will talk of each one making it easier to spot when you are being manipulated.

You will also gain valuable information on signs that your new partner is a narcissist and why you have chosen them. There is certainly a difference between healthy and non-healthy dates when we can recognize the differences, and it can save a lot of pain and heartache in the future.

This is only a look at the many pieces of dating a narcissist that will be covered inside. Take your time as you work through it, and it is amazing how much better protected you and your heart will be. You will also find that you are ready to stand up for yourself and move away from the toxicity of narcissism.

There are plenty of books on this subject on the market, thanks again for choosing this one! Every effort was made to ensure it is full of as much useful information as possible; please enjoy!

# Chapter 1

# The 3 Cycles of Narcissistic Abuse

Narcissists use a specific cycle of events, and it can be seen in just about every relationship that they enter into. The abuse is clear and the process is difficult. It leaves the other party feeling awful, and oftentimes takes a lot of effort for them to fully recover. Obviously, any type of abuse is not good, and the abuse of the narcissist is even worse. They use a variety of different tactics to make you feel crazy and if you can't function without them.

The three cycles of narcissistic abuse are idealizing, devaluation, and discarding. You must understand that at the core of narcissistic personality disorder is the inability to truly bond and attach to other people.

This relationship cycle is demonstrated frequently in narcissists because of this reason. Their patterns will be repeated with each relationship that they enter into, and it is exceptionally unfortunate for the party that actually falls in love with them.

## Idealize

The first step in the narcissistic abuse cycle is idealizing. This is going to be the stage of your relationship where everything seems just right or at least on the surface it does. When a narcissist targets someone, they will make them feel as if they are the most special thing ever to exist. They will be completely infatuated with you.

This can stage of their cycle is very confusing as it looks just like love. However, if you take a closer look, likely you will be able to see it is more obsession than anything else. Narcissists are not stable emotionally, so their ability to provide another person with actual love is practically impossible. They will not be able to sustain a relationship that is healthy and full of love, support, and stability.

Narcissists are always seeking approval. They need people to give them a lot of attention to help secure themselves in who they are. They have a constant need to have their egos stroked. When they enter into a new relationship, it is the perfect time to find the satisfaction that they crave. All relationships go through a honeymoon period, where things are new and exciting. Each party's attention is focused on the other person, and this gives the narcissist a bigger thrill than most.

When the narcissist picks a new lover, they will shower them with attention. Oftentimes, they will tell them that they are smarter, better looking, nicer, or more successful than anyone else they have ever been with. They will build you up so that you feel you are one of the best people on the planet. It's amazing how great the narcissist is at convincing themselves of these things, even if they only last for a short period of time. Sure, we all have good qualities, but what the narcissist does and how they make you feel goes way beyond pointing out your good qualities.

They will make you look grandiose in every way, and this can be very appealing to most people. They prey on every type of person, and let's face it, who doesn't love a compliment coming from someone we have newly found interest in. The real problem is the compliments are being made so that the narcissist can feel better about themselves.

The narcissist will build their new partner up in every way. It helps inflate both people's egos. The narcissist needs to feel superior, and they also know it will help draw in their new love interest.

Narcissists don't care about the person's soul, nature, or whether or not they are compatible. They are more focused on things like looks, money, and people that are kind in nature or have a hard time saying no.

They are the perfect targets. The narcissist will be looking for traits that make them feel good, and of course, everything at the beginning of a relationship is heightened, making it seem even better to them. This, unfortunately, does not last, nor can you build a lasting relationship on it.

When you fall for the flattery of a narcissist, it is dangerous. They idealize or love bomb you to make you feel as if you are the most important person in their world. You will likely be showered with gifts, kind words, and excellent sexual relations.

All of these things make it very easy to fall for the narcissist. It is important to note that the idealizing stage is also oftentimes referred to as the love bombing stage. As you can easily see, that is exactly what the narcissist is doing, bombing their potential partner with love.

Many people find comfort and relief when they find the person that treats them this way. They may actually believe that they have found the person they are meant to be with. This makes things even more devastating when it all eventually falls apart. This stage of the narcissistic cycle of abuse can last for days, weeks, months, and in some extraordinary cases, even years.

When you speak with people who have survived narcissistic abuse and have found the strength to get away from it, they will frequently tell you that they believed that they had found their soulmate. Someone who understood them on the ultimate level and made them feel admired, understood, and supported in ways they did not believe was possible. The narcissist is a master of making people feels this way, and it can make it insanely hard to see what is really happening.

This stage of the cycle is meant to get you hooked, and it works more often than not. It tends to lead to co-dependency, which is exactly what the narcissist wants and needs.

Your attention is needed by the narcissist to keep their ego boosted, and you, in turn, need their affection and, eventually, their approval. The narcissist will prey on your fears and weaknesses to ensure they get the end result that they want, control over you and your life.

# Devaluation

The next stage in their vicious cycle is the devaluation stage. After the narcissist has made you trust them and become open with them, the cycle of devaluation will begin. It typically overlaps the love-bombing phase, which makes this a very confusing time for the person that has fallen for a narcissist. A lot of times, the devaluation stage won't be noticed in the beginning because you are still so in love and enthralled by your partner.

When you have entered into this stage of the cycle, you will start to see through actions and words that what the narcissist used to proclaim about you as wonderful isn't what they felt at all. You will start to see how many lies have been told. It is very likely that their behavior will change quite a bit. The narcissist feels safe to be their true self, and they feel confident that they will be able to hold power over you and take complete control.

You may notice that they don't actually have a concern about whether or not you are ok, even if you are facing a serious illness or a life-threatening situation. If you are distressed or in need of help, they will no longer be available.

In short, your importance as a person in their life will no longer be easily seen, if it can be seen at all. Instead of things feeling great, you will start to notice that things simply aren't the same, and they feel off.

Where they were once caring and compassionate, they are now aloof to your existence. They are starting to show negative attention. The narcissist is feeling bored in this stage as the initial heightened emotions wear off. They start to question your worthiness, and they start to question you about it.

If you start to feel as if your relationship is off and you can't discuss it with your partner in a way that helps to solve the problem, you should not ignore it. Your body is trying to inform you that you are in danger. It can be easy to ignore this as the last fill in the blank amount of time has been glorious with your partner; however, you should never ignore your instincts, it is uncommon for them to steer you in the wrong direction.

As the partner of a narcissist, you will likely justify a lot of things to yourself at first, and then depending on how far it goes, to others, as well. As human beings, we are exceptionally good at rationalizing things. It is a coping mechanism that is tragically skewed.

The process of the narcissist is slow. You will only notice small things for quite some time, and this is why their tactics work so well. Your faith in them is only being taken away from a tiny piece at a time.

As things continue, they will likely start to verbally abuse you. This is when gaslighting tactics, accusations, extreme mood swings, and even cheating will likely occur. They will intentionally do things to make you feel confused. We will look at the narcissistic harem later on in this book, where you will learn more about the tricks the narcissist uses to gain control.

As you may already know, the narcissist will be unable to take any sort of blame. So, when you try and let them know they made a mistake, you will be greeted with criticism and denial. The less you stroke their ego, the more they will start to stroke their own. You will see them boasting more. Their behavior around other people as compared to when you are alone will be quite different, as well. It is certainly a sign that something is seriously wrong.

As noted, this process does not happen overnight. Over a period of time, you will bond with the narcissist in a way that makes you think you need them in your life. This could be for strength, support, or love.

There are an endless number of reasons you may feel as if you can't live without this person in your life. With this bond, you have to them, and they will manipulate you. The bonding is required because otherwise, no one would stick around long enough for them to gain true control.

They will make you feel powerless without them, and this type of bonding is referred to as *trauma bonding*. The narcissist will cut you down just to "save" you by picking you back up. They will attack your looks, job capability, intelligence, and anything else they think will make you more vulnerable and malleable towards them. When the narcissist is being kind or showing compassion, it will make their partner feel relief and keep them in the web questioning if they really are the ones to blame.

The longer this goes on, the worse the outcome is going to be. The victim will have their mind twisted without even realizing it. They will likely cut people out of their lives and solely focus on the narcissist. They will lose their sense of self and their sense of purpose. They may start questioning their own reality and only put trust and faith into what the narcissist has to say.

People that care about the victim will start to see the changes.

It is likely that they are going to try and talk with their loved one about what they are obviously seeing, but the victim will likely be unable to see it. In fact, they will likely make up excuses and defend the narcissist as they are completely enthralled and under the belief that they need the narcissist abuser in their life. If continuously pressed, the victim will go to extremes to keep the narcissist. They will cut important people completely out of their lives, and the narcissist will encourage it.

One of the most important things to remember about the devaluation stage is that the narcissist will prey on your weaknesses and insecurities. This means it is going to look different for every person, but the process is still the same. Find a way to make you feel inferior beyond belief and keep you to a chain that is closely tethered to the narcissist's leg. This is done so their ego can be built, and yours can be crushed.

## Discard

The final phase in the narcissist's cycle of abuse is the discard phase. This is the time that they no longer have any use for you.

The only purpose you ever served for them was to provide them with the attention they need to feel in control and superior. This attention and energy help the narcissist keep ahold of their false self.

When the narcissist doesn't believe the attention you are giving them is enough or if you have threatened their image too many times, they start to look for other places to get what they need. They will get distracted by other people more easily. They will also boast about themselves more than ever. It is also likely they will tear you down in front of others whether you are there or not.

Once the wrath of the narcissist has started, it is going to seem as if it is impossible to stop. Many people find the discard phase happens after standing up for themselves too many times. It also often occurs after the narcissist feels that you have defended yourself against their beliefs too many times. There are also times it happens for no apparent reason, the important thing to remember is this can be a truly ugly experience.

It is important to note that just because your relationship with the narcissist is in the discard phase, does not mean it is over.

Narcissists thrive on other people's pain. It shows that others are lesser, and it somehow helps them concrete the idea that they are special. They believe it concretes the idea for others as well. This could mean that the narcissist comes in and out of your life. They may disappear for days or weeks at a time just to show up on your doorstep with roses. You must remember that this is all a game to them, and they will do their best to keep you playing for as long as possible.

They prey on you even more if they find out you are seriously hurting since they left. If you reach out to them or talk about them to mutual friends and they find out, you will be fueling their narcissistic fire. They will continue to find joy and energy in your pain and suffering. The narcissist knows that by letting go of you, it will cause a great amount of pain.

The high that the narcissist gets from your pain is fleeting. This is why they continue to hurt you over and over. They feel validated in their false ego each time they show power over another person. You must remember that the narcissist is not a full person; they function with an emptiness that must always be filled to continue to have the illusion of being full.

In the discard phase, the narcissist may start off small before finally leaving. They may start by giving you the silent treatment.

The only responses that they have to give you will be demeaning. There will be a heaviness and tension in the air around them all the time. You will constantly feel like you are doing something wrong, even if you are doing nothing at all. This silent treatment will likely be paired with them ignoring you completely. Many find that they are also apt to start humiliating you regardless of who is around, and they tend to stray to other lovers more frequently and with no regard to whether you know about it or not.

When you go through something like this, feeling as if you love someone, it is traumatizing. It will be difficult for them to find closure of any sort. The back and forth of the narcissist is very difficult to deal with. They will treat you absolutely terribly or ignore you completely just to turn around and act like they are remorseful and want to fix what was broken in the relationship. They are trying to squeeze every last bit of energy out of you that they can.

One of the saddest parts of all of this is the fact that the narcissist intentionally did things to make you feel this way. They slowly but surely pulled the wool over your eyes. It is done this way so that they feel powerful. As long as you will continue to let the cycle happen, the narcissist will keep playing along. It gives them exactly what they want.

When you are the one that decides to leave the narcissist instead of them leaving you, it is a completely different ball game. They will do any and everything they can to try and ruin your life. Some may spread lies about you while others may go to the point of stalking you. They want to show you that they still hold the power to control you and your life.

Cutting the narcissist out of your life completely is one of the only ways to end this phase. Many people choose to change their phone numbers, email address, and block the narcissist from their social media feeds. This is obviously going to lessen the ways they have to get to you, but be careful as narcissists tend to be crafty and may find other ways to get into contact with you. If they do, use your head and don't fall for their tactics.

# Chapter 2

# The Overt & Covert Narcissist

People that have narcissistic personality disorder will fall into one of two subtypes. They will be in the subtype of Overt Narcissism of Covert Narcissism. There are a few similarities between the two, but in reality, they are quite different. All narcissists tend to be conceited; they have a complete disregard for others and have problems with self-indulgence. In this chapter, we are going to go over overt and covert narcissism. Once you have a good understanding of each of them, it will make it easier to identify the narcissist that may be trying to creep their way into your life.

Inside of this chapter, we are also going to take a look at the type of manipulation tactics the narcissist will use while dating someone.

When you can recognize the signs of a narcissist, you will be able to set yourself free from them before the damage starts. Getting out early is the best way to handle a narcissistic relationship. The manipulation will start from day one, and we are going to clue you in on the signs of it, so you won't be taken advantage of to later have your life completely destroyed.

# The Overt Narcissist

Let's start by talking about the overt narcissist. The overt narcissist is the one that is flashy and showy. They live a life of grandeur. Around others, they are constantly in need of looking like a hero. They must be outstanding and successful in every area of life, and they will do anything they can to make sure you see it. This can be their lovemaking skill, attractiveness, wealth, and power.

The overt narcissist has an inflated sense of self-importance. They think they are unique, and they are very special. The only people that could possibly understand the overt narcissist, in their eyes, are others that are special or hold a high status in life. Even their smallest achievements, they believe, should be looked at as outstanding feats.

This type of narcissist will exaggerate everything. This is especially true of things they feel they are talented at. They have an expectation that people will look at them as if they are superior. This is due to the fact that they truly believe that they are superior. Some common adjectives used to describe the overt narcissist are:

- Pretentious

- Boastful

- Conceded

- Self-centered

- Self-absorbed

- Entitled

Obviously, none of these are the best adjectives to describe a person; however, when it comes to the overt narcissist, they are absolutely true. They believe that they deserve favorable treatment regardless of what they are doing. No matter how big or how small their accomplishment they will find a way to make whatever they did the best thing that could have ever happened, and you better not forget it only happened that way because they were the ones who did it.

The overt narcissists need or adoration unparalleled. They will continuously put themselves in situations where they can be in the spotlight. This allows their need of attention to be sated, at least for a short while.

When the overt narcissist is not getting the attention and admiration, they think they deserve their behaviors to become quite distasteful. If they feel the focus of attention has shifted or if they are feeling scorned, they will act out by rejecting others and being scornful in return. They always need to be the best and will act as a child would if they feel any other way.

The overt narcissist does not have any problem exploiting others so that they can meet their own desires. They have a sense of arrogance by which you have likely never experienced before. It is likely they will hide behind a mask of humility, but it is exceptionally false. They do not have empathy, nor do they take the time to try and understand what other people need.

The overt narcissist deals with a lot of conflicting emotions. They, under the façade, feel that they are worthless, and this tends to make them envious of people that do well in life. The outside shows that they believe they are the best and that everyone should be envious of them.

With these conflicting feelings, they are unable to trust others, and they typically feel threatened. The more threatened they feel, the better the likelihood of an emotional or physical eruption is going to happen.

Wanting everything other people have that holds value is another trait of the overt narcissist. They will manipulate people to gain information, fame, knowledge, power, or even positions. When they have what others have, they feel more powerful.

The overt narcissist is great at modeling the behaviors of people whom they admire.

They will pretend that the façade is their own when realistically, it is not at all. Fraudulent personalities are very common in overt narcissists. They will say they have made great achievements, like gaining degrees, awards, or accreditations, even if there is absolutely no truth to it. The narcissist has no problems telling lies.

The reactions of the overt narcissist can be pretty extreme. Their ego and sense of self-importance are over-inflated, and it shows anytime they are contradicted, criticized, or they lose at something. When this happens, the negative response will be impossible to miss.

They will lash out in one way or another. It is important to note that when the overt narcissist is in public, they will do their best to appear calm, cool, and collected at all times. It will take quite a bit to make them drop this display and allow their rage to flow, but it does happen.

If the overt narcissist does lose control in front of other people, it can leave them feeling extremely ashamed. They may go through deep bouts of depression, and they may even have suicidal thoughts. Overt narcissists have major contradictions in regard to their relationship with themselves, ethics, ideals, standards, and the concept of self and social adaptations.

The overt narcissist can be easier to spot than the covert narcissist, but you must understand that they are well-versed when it comes to playing games with people. They are manipulative and good at taking control of a situation and of people. They will not show their hand easily, but with some decent observation skills, you will likely be able to start picking them out among the crowd.

## The Covert Narcissist

Now that we have gone over the ends and outs of the overt narcissist, we are going to take a close look at the covert narcissist. The covert narcissist does not have an adequate perception of themselves. They tend to be deflated and lacking in many of the areas that make the overt narcissist who they are. More often than not, they are not aggressive, and they don't participate in over the Top behaviors while in the public eye.

The covert narcissist is more apt to be depressed. They experience feelings of complete emptiness and consistently feel as if things are falling apart around them. This type of narcissist is also referred to as a vulnerable narcissist and sometimes as an introverted narcissist.

It can be extremely difficult to pick out the covert narcissist. Oftentimes it seems like they are humble, extremely shy, or anxious. They find gratification indirectly. They tend to take things personally when they shouldn't. This leads to feelings of being mistreated, misunderstood, and unappreciated. The covert narcissist is extremely distrustful.

They do not put a lot of value into themselves, but they do have dreams of grandeur. The covert narcissist often contemplates why they are misunderstood. Additionally, they can't understand why people don't appreciate them more.

The reason that they are still considered to have narcissistic personality disorder is due to the fact that they still desire admiration and have a need to feel as if they are special. They will be lacking in empathy, and they will have a sense of entitlement that is greater than most people. Just like the overt narcissist, they are self-centered and believe that they should receive special treatment from others.

The covert narcissist has feelings that they are simply misunderstood. That other people are not able to recognize how special they truly are. They believe they are extremely unique and that people are simply unable to recognize it. This type of narcissist is also excellent at being the victim or the martyr in any given situation.

You are likely to find the covert narcissist in a profession that helps other people. It may genuinely appear as if they care for others; however, the motivation toward why they are doing this type of job is completely different from someone who actually cares about other people.

They are looking for recognition, pride, and power through the means of helping others. Their form of help may be more like taking over without even being asked. Due to the fact that they think they are superior, they will behave self-righteously.

There are definitely some core traits between the overt and the covert narcissist that are the same. It simply looks a little bit different. Where the overt narcissist will have a need to be the center of attention, the covert will feel slighted when they are not. The covert will also play the role of the victim much more quickly if it means that they will get attention.

The covert narcissist won't work on charming his audience but instead will appear to be completely self-absorbed. They find other people to be ignorant and boring. Instead of passing orders on to people, they will use passive-aggressive behaviors to get what they want. Oftentimes they will agree to help with something or do something with no intention of actually following through.

They will make excuses like they forgot or pretend that they never agreed to it in the 1st place. You must remember that all narcissists are manipulative, and this is exactly what they're doing, trying to manipulate you.

Self-pity is another tool that the covert narcissist likes to use frequently.

Where the overt narcissist will put people down directly, the covert narcissist is more apt to display envy over others. As noted, it is all manipulation; it is simply the way they go about it that is different.

When you are dealing with a covert narcissist, they're not going to brag openly about their achievements. Their introverted nature is going to make them smugger and more judgmental. They tend to act disinterested and aloof. When you are dealing with a covert narcissist, they will have the tendency to seem bored. They will look away, yawn, sigh, or simply be impolite around others.

All narcissists will have bad reactions if they feel they are being criticized; however, the reaction of the covert narcissist is going to be the worst as they are extremely sensitive. Unlike the overt narcissist, they will not become aggressive; they will instead feel neglected or belittled.

They are prone to hypersensitivity and anxiety. Oftentimes they will feel as if the world is persecuting them.

It can be very difficult to spot the covert narcissist because they are passive. However, you must understand that they are just as difficult to deal with in a relationship, and the relationship will be just as toxic when you are with them or with an overt narcissist.

The covert narcissist's abuse is more subtle, making it harder to see. Just because it is subtle does not change the fact that it will wear you down and eventually completely destroy your sense of self and your sense of self-worth.

You will constantly be seeking their attention, and they will continuously ignore you. They suck you in by getting you to try and help and console them. You have to understand that inside of these people is a void that will never be filled no matter how hard you try. They will always have the mentality that they are the victim, and there is no way to change this. When people try, they typically end up with feelings of anger and resentment.

The lack of empathy that the covert narcissist has will make them unable to see you as an individual. They will do anything they have to, to gain and maintain control and power over you and the relationship.

Their wants and needs will always be more important than yours. Obviously, this is going to leave you feeling very lonely and neglected.

There are a few personality traits that can help you determine whether or not your new interest is a covert narcissist or not. Let's take a look at a list of characteristics that can help you understand what you may be dealing with.

If you see several of the following traits, there is a good chance you will want to end the relationship and move on right away. Look out for people that are:

- Extremely sensitive to criticism

- Passive-aggressive

- Putting themselves down frequently

- Shy and withdrawn from society

- Caught up in grandiose fantasies

- Frequently dealing with anxiety, depression, or feelings of nothingness

- Unable to let go of things and hold grudges for long periods of time

- Envious of others frequently

- Struggling with feelings of inadequacy consistently

- Only showing signs of empathy when it is self-serving

Obviously, each of us has flaws, and some of our flaws may fall into this list. It is when your prospective partner starts to tick multiple boxes that you need to start worrying about what is lying under their false presentation of themselves. If you are unsure about what you are witnessing, don't be afraid to take your time and really observe what is happening around you.

When we are mindful of our experiences, and we listen to our gut instinct, it can really help keep us away from emotionally devastating situations.

It is certainly harder to pick the covert narcissist out of the crowd, but that does not mean it can't be done. You simply need to do your research and take your time before jumping into anything serious with someone you just met. Listen to how they talk about other people, as well as how they talk about themselves. These will be your best clues, in the beginning, to try and understand what type of person you are actually dealing with.

# Manipulation Narcissists Use in Dating

Whether you are just starting to date, a narcissist, or the two of you have been dating for a while, and there are a variety of different manipulation tactics that they will use to start to gain power and control over you. Some of these manipulation tactics can be difficult to see but if you take time to reflect on each date you have with someone, it may be easier. Additionally, educating yourself by reading books like this one can help clue you in to what is actually going on right in front of you as compared to what it looks like.

One of the first things that the narcissist is going to do to manipulate you is to use the love-bombing tactic. This will be done early on in the relationship once they have picked their target. As previously noted, the narcissist is going to make you feel that there is no one on earth more special than you. As the victim, it is unfortunate because you will feel extremely lucky and alive after finding the person that just walked into your life.

You must understand that there is nothing pure about the intentions of the narcissist. They use love bombing to get you exactly where they want you so that they can take complete control and hold all of the power in your relationship.

This tactic is extremely smart as more often than not, and it leads to the victim actually believing they have done something wrong to make their loving and caring partner turn into such a monster. The victim will end up feeling trapped and do just about anything to bring back the partner that they had when they first met.

Another manipulation tactic that the narcissist will use is expressing gratitude. Realistically, they never actually feel genuine gratitude toward you. It is simply a tactic used to help you rationalize their bad behavior.

When the narcissist appears to understand when you do something right or come forward stating that they have done something wrong, it is not because they actually believe it. It is done so that they will continue to gain power and hold the upper hand by tricking you into thinking things are true that are absolutely untrue.

The narcissist will take time to make it look as if they're putting effort into their relationship with you. This will be a false effort, and it won't be with an ulterior motive. Narcissists understand that if it looks like they are trying; their partner will try even harder to reciprocate it.

Eventually, most people will be able to see what is happening, but it is not always the case when you are dealing with a narcissist. We say this because they will do a good job of showing their grandiose good behaviors and have an utter refusal to look at any of the behaviors that have that are bad. This can be extremely confusing to the person that is in a relationship with them. Oftentimes, the terrible behaviors are not recognized until you are farther into the relationship, and things are going tragically awry.

Narcissists are notoriously good with words. They will use them to their advantage in every way possible.
You will find that it doesn't matter what you say they will be able to put a twist or a spin on it, so it means what they want it to mean rather than what you actually meant. Just as narcissists are in love with themselves, they are also in love with using words against people. Their affluent language draws people in, and further down the road, it will be used to tear those same people apart.

Some of the manipulation that a narcissist uses is pretty common in most people. What we're talking about here is telling lies. The narcissist lies to themselves on a daily basis, so lying to you is no problem at all.

They will not feel remorse or regret when they tell lies. Actually, they will inflate their ego further when they feel as if they have pulled one over on someone as it helps concrete the idea that they are superior in every way.

Narcissists may also be extremely vague when they're trying to manipulate you. They do this so that they can have time to learn about you and figure out what it is that makes you tick so that they can use it against you. In the beginning, it may seem as if they are a good listener and that they are truly interested in what you have to say when in reality, they're simply doing research so that they can better manipulate you in the future.

You must understand that there are hundreds of different ways to manipulate people, and narcissists tend to be well versed in many of them. From flat out lies to simple exaggeration, they will do what it takes to suck you into the chaos that is being with a narcissist. Recognizing manipulation can be difficult, which is why it is always advantageous to take the time to truly get to know someone before you make a commitment to them. Obviously, we can all be fooled and tricked but the more you know the less chance of that happening there is. Manipulation is a nasty business, and it is one of the favorite tools of the narcissist. By getting familiar with it, you won't have to worry about being manipulated in the future.

# Chapter 3

# The Narcissist's Harem

As we all know, the narcissist needs people to constantly provide them with love and adoration. This supply of energy is what helps them maintain their false ego. One single person is not going to be able to give them all of the attention that they need, so they will include a variety of different people in their toxic lives to find the supply that they feel is required. You must always remember that the people the narcissist chooses are always replaceable, and their roles in the life of the narcissist can change very quickly. Each person that is in the web of the narcissist will constantly be battling to prove their value.

The narcissist's haram will be a group of people that fall into certain categories, and they all hold a different purpose in regard to the narcissist.

In this chapter, we are going to look over the 5 categories that you may fall into if you are part of the conglomeration that falls into the chaos of a narcissist.

In pretty much every relationship that a narcissist is involved, you will be able to pinpoint these people. After working your way through this chapter, you will be able to identify the role more easily you may be playing to the narcissist and the roles the other people that around you are playing.

The people that make up the narcissists harem can change from time to time. Realistically, anyone can be involved. This could be ex-partners, potential partners, family members, friends, or even coworkers. As long as the narcissist sees purpose in a person's ability to supply them with the attention that they seek, they are a possible target. Narcissists really do prefer to have a variety of options.

When the narcissist builds their harem, they will take time to do it. As with all things, it is something that they plan out. They seek out people that are giving and accommodating. If they notice someone is making excuses for other people or they can easily see a way in, they will use it to their advantage and find a way to add you to their regime.

Depending on the situation, the people involved with a narcissist may or may not know about one another.

If it is an intimate relationship, there is less likelihood of the members knowing about each other as this would allow them the opportunity to compare notes on the narcissist, and that could work out very badly for them. In a family situation or a work situation, it could be very likely that the people inside of the harem know about each other as it is not dangerous to the narcissist for this to be the case.

The attention and adoration that a narcissist seeks are like a drug to them. Just like drugs, eventually, the supply is not going to offer as much relief as it used to. As the newness of your interaction with the narcissist starts to wear off, they will move you around in the hierarchy so that they still have you there if they need you, but you will no longer be the newest and best thing, but they're focused on.

Just as hoarders keep items forever for fear that they will need them someday, narcissists do the same but with people. Regardless of how many times the narcissist has hurt you, they will find ways to work themselves back into your life so that they can keep a hold of you. Obviously, this is not for your sake but for theirs. If they have any feelings that they still have to use for you, they will do everything they can to make sure you are right there when they need you.

Now that we have looked at some of the ideas behind the narcissistic harem come on, let's take a look at the different roles that are located inside of it and what each 1 means. Remember that you could change frequently between the 5 different roles just depending on the worthiness that the narcissist places on you. It is also important to note that the feelings surrounding a narcissistic harem can be very similar to those that are involved when someone joins a cult. Just like a cult, it can be very hard to see what is happening right in front of your eyes due to manipulation and promises of grandeur.

The first position is going to be held by the newest target of their love-bombing tactics. As previously discussed, the narcissist, when they find a new interest, will bombard that person with love, affection, and support. This lures them into the trap the narcissist has set and gives them false belief in how the narcissist feels about them. This person could be a new potential partner, but it could also be a child within the narcissist's family, someone new the narcissist is working with, or simply a person that has entered into the clique of the narcissist.

The narcissist gains a variety of different people that will offer them admiration so that they have the supply that they need.

So, once you have become the focus of the narcissist, they're going to do everything they can to get you into this group with their other admirers. They want you to be ready to provide them with attention at a moment's notice. If you take the time to look, a narcissist tends to hang around their ex-lovers more than most people would. This is due to the fact that they will not get rid of a person if they still feel they have use for them.

The narcissist will spend all of their time doting on their newest target so that the victim will willingly step into their circle. The narcissist also does this so that they can flaunt their newest toy in front of the old toys that they have laid to the side. This new person in their life can do nothing wrong in their eyes, and the narcissist will be laser-focused on them. Typically, this means that they are going to at least have a period of time where they are excluding the other people that are members of their toxic harem.

It is important to remember that love bombing is very hard to recognize. Most people don't see red flags when a new potential person in their life is providing them with flattery, praise, support, and admiration.
These things help concrete the fact that you will end up being a part of the narcissist's grand scheme.

When you are the target of their love-bombing, it is likely that the other members of the harem are going to be envious or jealous of your current standing. This could lead to them trying to sabotage you in life or simply in the eyes of the narcissist. You must realize that even if they are not able to bring you down a notch in the narcissist's eyes, it will happen eventually anyway. Things that are new will eventually become old, and the narcissist will knock you down many pegs to simply replace you with a shiny new toy.

The next slot in the narcissistic harem is that of the enabler. Many times they are referred to as flying monkeys. People gain this position with the narcissist when they are truly devoted to them and their way of thinking. They will defend the narcissist to the very end, regardless of the bad behaviors the narcissist shows. Additionally, they help the narcissist refrain from taking accountability for their actions.

The enabler will do just about anything the narcissist tells them to do. If told to lie, they will do it without question. If you are in the position of being an enabler, you will shut other people down if they try and speak poorly of the narcissist in your life.

Some will even go to extremes when it comes to the way they defend their narcissist, which could lead to a variety of negative situations for everyone that is involved.

The narcissist may encourage their enablers to bully, harass, or taunt people if the narcissist finds them threatening in any way. The enabler is so blind to the tactics of the narcissist that they will willingly do these things to help protect them. No matter what the narcissist has on their agenda, the flying monkeys will support it without question.

Pretty much anyone can fall into this group. The narcissist will use their spouse, siblings, parents, friends, or even their coworkers if they feel they will provide them with the services they need from an enabler. It is interesting to know that even people the narcissist does not know very well, can end up being one of their flying monkeys by simply listening and following what the narcissist does without much question in the beginning.

After the enabler comes the right-hand man. More often than not, this person is going to have traits of a sociopath or a psychopath as well. The person that falls into this role is likely someone that has been around for a very long time and isn't going anywhere anytime soon. They will likely hold the same values and ideals as the narcissist.

While many of the roles in the narcissist's harem are interchangeable, this one is typically filled by the same person, and it is very unlikely that that is going to change.

The type of support that the narcissist gets from their right-hand man is a bit different than the adoration and attention that they get from everyone else. The right-hand man typically has the same nature as the narcissist. They tend to be ruthless and without empathy. They will work with the narcissist on all of their agendas, and this is something the narcissist cannot easily replace.

In the narcissistic harem, the right-hand man is likely the longest standing member. The narcissist holds them in very high regard. There are a variety of different roles that this person may play in the narcissist life; however, more often than not, they are the narcissist's best friend. They are also, typically, the person that the narcissist confides in and schemes with. The narcissist and their right-hand man are co-conspirators in just about everything that they do. It is possible that this role could change should the narcissist find someone that they feel fits into this rank better, but it is very unlikely.

The 4th position of the narcissistic harem is that of the empathetic caretaker.
Narcissists will find people that are exceptionally compassionate and empathetic just so that they can take advantage of them.

When it comes to trauma bonding, these people have it the absolute worst. They are under a completely unrealistic belief that the narcissist cares about them. They are devoted and deluded. It is likely they believe the narcissist is a truly good person who is simply misunderstood.

People with high levels of empathy are oftentimes the most acceptable to fall into the web of lies that the narcissist creates. Don't forget that a narcissist is great at playing the victim. When someone has a great capacity for empathy, the narcissist will notice it and utilized this to their advantage. They can use this in a variety of different ways. For example, the empathetic caretaker will be approachable and may be able to bring new people into the fold of the narcissist's harem with ease. It is easy to trust and open up to an empathetic person, so they are able to ensnare people more easily than the narcissist themselves.

Not only is the empathetic caretaker good at luring new victims into the narcissist's web of deceit they're also good at stroking the ego of the narcissist and making them feel better. If the narcissist is feeling some sort of emotional need, it is likely that they will turn to the empathetic caretaker to state that need.

Unfortunately, the empathetic caretaker will fall for it each and every time, providing the narcissist with what they feel is reciprocated compassion, kindness, and caring even though it is only one-sided.

This position in the hair room is critical. The empathetic caretaker helps uphold the image that the narcissist is a good and decent person. Without an empathetic caretaker, people would more easily become wise to the conniving in nefarious ways of the narcissist. When the narcissist surrounds themselves with people that are compassionate and empathetic, it helps them to fool everyone else into thinking that they are the same. This is a great facade that can keep others from seeing the true nature of the narcissist.

The last position in the narcissistic harem is referred to as the scapegoat. This may be the last position to fill, but it is also one of the most important ones. The scapegoat is a target for all things negative to both the narcissist and their harem. Emotionally this person will be taken advantage of more so than anyone else. They will be persecuted and subjected to a variety of different heinous acts. The narcissist will intentionally neglect or ignore them while providing other people within the group praise.

If you are in the position of being the scapegoat in the narcissistic harem, it is likely that you feel as if you are completely invisible. It is also likely that you feel you are disposable not only to the narcissist but in general. The bad behaviors, failures, or shortcomings of the narcissist will all be pushed on to the scapegoat.

The position of the scapegoat is one that changes more frequently than the other positions. Pretty much any member of the narcissistic harem can become a scapegoat at any time. The moment the narcissist feels that you have outlived your usefulness, it is likely that they are going to put you into the position of the scapegoat. You may not stay in this position forever, but it is likely that if a narcissist is in your life, you will fall into this category more than once. This is especially true if you're the type of person that will challenge the narcissist or stand up for yourself on a frequent basis.

The narcissist runs on a cycle, so shifting between the person being love-bombed to being pushed down to the scapegoat position is not uncommon. Realizing what is happening as you experience; all of this is extremely difficult. The narcissist looks at you as if you are a puppet, and they are your master.

This means they can play with you whenever they decide they want to but the moment they get bored, they will toss you into the corner and look for something new that provides a different type of stimulation that they find better. However, the moment they start to get bored with the new item it is very likely that they will pick you back up, dust you off, and make you feel like the most special person in the world so that you will stay right where they want you, under their thumb.

Many people that are in the narcissistic cycle start to believe that the things that are happening to them are their fault. This is horrifically untrue. The wires inside of a narcissist are crossed, and their behaviors are their own fault. They are great in the ways of manipulation trickery. This is how they get people to start to believe that they are the problem rather than understanding that the narcissist is the problem.

This cycle and hierarchy with the narcissist are never going to change. It is part of the problem when you get into a relationship with a narcissist is that you believe you may be able to help them make changes for the better. All this does is prolong your exposure to them, which gets you in deeper and deeper, making it exceptionally difficult to get out of the toxic situation that you are facing. While you are looking at how this is impacting your life and others, the narcissist is playing a game.

Replacing people for different and interesting options will always happen, but don't be surprised when they eventually come back to you searching for the source of power that you want to supply them and will likely end up supplying them again.

As with all things in regard to dealing with a narcissist, if you are within their harem, it's going to be exceptionally hard to see. Your friends and family may be the 1st to try and clue you in that there's something wrong in your friendship or relationship with a certain person, but it is unlikely that you'll be willing to hear what they have to say or accept it. The only true way to protect yourself from becoming part of the narcissist's harem is to understand what it is and take a step back to really evaluate things before committing yourself to another person.

Unfortunately, there are a lot of people in the world that have nefarious intent and are more than willing to take advantage of a kind and empathetic people. Being present in the moment and being mindful of what is occurring around you are your best defenses. If you believe that someone you are involved in one way or another is a narcissist, the best thing you can do is take a giant step back before they suck you into the chaos that is their lives.

Even if their friends and the people closest to them are telling you how great they are going with your gut and listen to the people that you genuinely trust before you do something, you can't take back and end up in the narcissistic house of horrors.

# Chapter 4

# Dating a Narcissist

You may have been on many dates with a narcissist and never recognized it. If you were lucky, the date did not go well, and you were able to get away from the person before they turned your life into total chaos. One of the best ways to spot a narcissist is to recognize the signs of one. In this chapter, we're going to look at a variety of different signs that can help you understand whether or not you are in the presence of a narcissist.

Many people don't realize that there may be reasons that they are drawn to narcissists. You may actually have a pattern of entering into this type of toxic relationship without ever being able to see that that is the case. So, we will also look at a variety of reasons that you may be drawn to and dating narcissists. Sometimes when you understand what is going on with yourself internally, it can help protect you from continuously making decisions that can tear your life apart.

# Signs of Narcissism

In today's world, people use the term narcissist all the time but realistically have no idea what it means. Narcissism is a mental condition that affects the person all the way through. They have a personality disorder. So, while there may be many people you know who are full of themselves or have a huge personality, it does not mean they are actual narcissists.

It can be very hard to spot a narcissist. This is especially true if you don't know much about them and you don't know what you're looking for. So, in this section of the book, we're going to give you a variety of different signs that can help you pinpoint when you are dealing with a narcissist. If a lot of these signs are prevalent with someone you have taken an interest in, it is a good idea to take a step back and evaluate whether going forward with them or not is a good plan. Welcoming a narcissist into your life will likely lead to chaos and abuse. The best advice we can give you is that if you come into contact with a narcissist, turn around and walk the other way so that they do not have a chance to get their hooks into you.

When you are dealing with a narcissist, they believe that they are better than everyone in pretty much any way possible. It is likely that they even believe they are above the law.

Due to the fact that they have such a complex of superiority, they will not see boundaries as something to respect, but they will see them as challenges. The narcissist will take pleasure in using manipulation to move around or past these boundaries. If you are investing your time in someone that always believes they are the exception to rules, it is one of the first signs that you are dealing with a narcissist.

Another great sign to show that you are dealing with a narcissist is sitting back and listening to the way a person speaks. As always, the narcissist needs attention so they will spend a lot of time talking about themselves. When they are talking about themselves. It will always be exaggerated, making them look like they are better than everyone else because, in their eyes, they are.

Narcissists are known for taking control of pretty much every conversation. They believe that what they have to say is more important than what anyone else has to say. Oftentimes, they will change the topic so that they can include information on their achievements or accomplishments. They will also try to add in information on any activity, issue, or concern that may provide them with the attention that they are seeking.

As you listen to what the narcissist has to say, you should try and pay attention to how they talk about other people.

What you will find when dealing with a narcissist is that they love to put other people down as it helps to build them up. They will likely be extremely focused on how people look or on the material possessions that they have. Anytime the narcissist has an opportunity to make others look less than, they will. So, by simply listening, you can learn a lot and save yourself a lot of trouble later on down the road.

During the initial moments of a relationship with a narcissist, they will likely come across as charming and attractive. This is due to the fact that they're trying to guarantee themselves the wind when it comes to you. Using charisma and flattery, they will gain your attention and make you feel extremely special. From there, they will try to seduce you so that they can start to take control. When you start to trust them, they will then begin to persuade and manipulate you so that they can reach their overall goals regardless of if yours align with theirs or not.

This sign is a bit difficult to see because the beginning of many relationships goes through a honeymoon period that looks very similar to the beginning of a relationship with a narcissist. There is nothing wrong with people being charismatic, complementary, or romantic.

However, the intent behind the narcissist's use of these things is completely different than those who do not suffer from this type of personality disorder. So, understand that this sign can be a bit difficult to peg, but when it is paired with other items on the list, it can give you a true judgment as to whether you are dealing with a narcissist or not.

The next way that you can spot a narcissist is to remember that they are not very reliable people, and it is rare for them to follow through. Words typically come easy to the narcissist, so you will want to pay attention to their actions as those speak much louder. When you are dealing with a narcissist, it is likely they are going to not show up when they said they were going to, or they will make agreements or promises that inevitably fall through.

They are not only unreliable in everyday life; they are also unreliable emotionally. If your prospective partner is there for you this moment and then absent the next time you need them, it is a decent sign that you are dealing with a narcissist. This is especially true if you step back and start to see a pattern. A pattern of inconsistency is a pretty clear sign, and it is also simple to see as long as you take the time to truly look at your situation.

If you see someone who constantly expects to be instantly gratified, it's a good sign that they may have narcissistic traits. Narcissists are known for being insanely self-centered and self-absorbed. This means if their needs are not being met instantaneously, they are not going to take it very well. They will put pressure on you to respond to them immediately and to do things exactly the way that they like them to be done.

This facet of the narcissist is actually pretty easy to test. The next time your prospective partner makes a request that doesn't make you comfortable, simply say no or ask them to give you time to consider it. Then take the time to notice how they respond and react to you. Take notice if they continue to try and persuade you or if they start to get angry, impatient, or irritated. If they do, there is a better likelihood that you are dealing with a narcissist, then you may have initially believed.

While this test is pretty fantastic, you also have to be aware that narcissists will go to great lengths to protect their false ego. When you first start seeing a narcissist and going on dates with them, they will do their best to be on the strictest of good behaviors. They do this to help ensure that they will get you on their side and be able to eventually prey upon you. So, it is best if you try this test more than once to see if their pleasant reaction is consistent or if they were just mustering it up to fool you.

Narcissists also have an extreme sense of entitlement. They expect that they will be treated better than others and that they deserve to be treated better than others. Their belief is that their needs should be catered to and that there is no need to return this type of attention. If you observe your date treating the waitstaff or other service people poorly, it is a bad sign. You should take notice of behaviors like ordering people around or pointing out even the smallest flaws in the people surrounding you. While doing this, the narcissist is also going to act high and mighty. Generally, people tend to be pretty kind to the service workers that are helping them. The narcissist simply won't be able to do this, and they will show you this side of themselves quicker than you may expect.

Obviously, manipulation is one of the very first signs that may be recognizable when dealing with a narcissist. They will twist people's thoughts and ideas in an unreasonable fashion to serve their own desires. Not only will they quickly start trying to take advantage of you, but they will also take advantage of other people. If you notice that your new love interest flaunts the fact that they have taken advantage of somebody or they have manipulated them so that they get their own desired outcome, it is not a good sign. Here again, truly listening to the person that you are starting to take an interest in can give you great insight as to the type of person you are dealing with.

Another sign that you are dealing with a narcissist is that they will constantly be putting other people down. In trying to always find superiority, they will put others down to relieve them of feelings of insecurity or inadequacy. The belief of the narcissist is that by putting other people down, they will build themselves up in the eyes of the people they are trying to take advantage of.

When they start putting other people down, they may be talking about coworkers, friends, relatives, or even people they were formerly in relationships with. When you first step into a relationship with a narcissist, it is likely that they are going to be very charming and provide you with many compliments. Instead of paying attention to these compliments, take the time to actually here the type of jokes and comments that they are making about you either in front of your face or in the background. What may initially sound like a joke could actually be a passive-aggressive poke to see how malleable you are and if they're going to be able to take advantage of you.

The offhanded comments and jokes that the narcissist makes that you should especially pay attention to are ones that are about your physique, clothing, background, job, and priorities.

The remarks that they make on these areas can be extremely telling. While a certain amount of playful comments can be accepted, they should not be cruel, and they should not attack your thoughts, feelings, or ideas.

The reaction of a narcissist when they don't get what they want will be much more extreme than it would with someone who was not narcissistic. Narcissists don't handle rejection or disappointment very well. When the person you are interested in doesn't get what they want, and they react with tantrums, personal attacks, judgment, and ridicule, it is a good sign that you might be dealing with a narcissist. They may also become extremely passive-aggressive, which means using things like the silent treatment against you. One last thing that the narcissist will do when told no is used emotional coercion. Emotional coercion is when somebody tries to blame you, calls you ungrateful, tries to guilt-trip you, or withholds intimacy intentionally.

The last sign that we're going to discuss that conclude you in to whether or not you are starting to date a narcissist is the inability to commit to you for a serious relationship. If you have been dating somebody for a while and they simply can't make a commitment, you should likely be concerned.

Sure, there are a lot of different reasons that people won't commit to a serious relationship, but when that is paired with one or more of the signs above, it is a reasonable conclusion that you're dealing with a narcissist.

If you're with someone who refuses to commit, you should take the time to hear them out. There are a plethora of reasons that they may be unwilling to commit, and many of those reasons are understandable. Narcissists are unable to commit because they are always on the lookout for a new and better player for their game.

We have provided you with a variety of different signs that the person you are getting into a relationship is a narcissist; however, you must understand that they may not show you any of these signs in the beginning. Narcissists are masters of manipulation, and they're always thinking one step ahead. They will do anything it takes to preserve their image, which includes using lies and deceit. So, pay attention to your gut instinct and take things slow so that you can make an educated decision on whether or not entering into a relationship with your new interest is worth it or not.

# Reasons You May Be Dating a Narcissist

There are a lot of people that feel as if narcissists are drawn to them like magnets. It may not be that narcissists are more drawn to you, but you may be more at holding on to them. For instance, many people that can easily see the negative attributes of a narcissist such as their need to be the center of attention, the constant reassurance they are seeking, or the sensitivity they have to be slighted. When they see these things, they may not recognize them as narcissistic traits, but they are still unfavorable. Due to the fact that these are unfavorable traits, most people will not go any further with the relationship.

People are often disturbed by the types of behaviors that the narcissist displays. They will disengage themselves from the situation because it is easier than trying to deal with someone who is difficult from the very beginning. The people that tend to stick around the narcissist will handle this type of situation in a very different way.

If you are a person that feels like narcissists are constantly drawn to you, you might need to take a look at your standards for relationships and what behaviors you will and will not tolerate.

To understand whether or not your standards are healthy and will keep you protected, you can ask yourself the following questions.

- At any point in time, have you ended a relationship because of selfishness on your partner's behalf?

- Are you able to set clear boundaries and stick to them?

- Do you know what behaviors in a relationship you will tolerate, and which ones are totally unacceptable?

- Do you rationalize staying in a bad relationship because you believe it can get better? Is this because of the way things started out in your relationship?

- Do you allow your partners to devalue you?

- Is making excuses for your partner's bad behavior commonplace?

- Have you put up with mental, physical, or emotional abuse without leaving?

If you do find that these questions relate to you, it is time to sit back and really look over your standards. You need to find strategies that will help weed out people with bad behaviors before they sink their claws into you.

Exiting a relationship because you feel that someone is taking advantage of you or that they have nefarious intent is not wrong. It may seem difficult to weed out the narcissists, but when you give people too many chances, you are simply giving them more time to manipulate and take advantage of you.

There are also a few different personality traits that narcissists will pick up on and try to take advantage of. Certain traits are found to be more useful to narcissists than others. So, if you are extremely empathetic, have a desire to help others, you are willing to try harder than most to make relationships work, or your sense of responsibility is strong, you are likely the perfect target for a narcissist.

All of these traits fall into the desires of a narcissist. They will do everything they can to take advantage of your kindness, compassion, and empathy. Most people don't try and hide these positive attributes that they hold. Unfortunately, with this, the narcissist is able to pick their target quite easily.

Narcissists also genuinely enjoy taking advantage of truly intelligent people. Everything in their lives is a game, and roping someone into their game that is smart feels like a major win for the narcissist. The high they get from besting an intelligent person is better than many others.

It's unfortunate because many intelligent people end up being taken advantage of without realizing what is going on before it is way too late, and they have suffered at the hands of the narcissist for far too long.

People that have lived through narcissistic abuse will oftentimes question themselves. The narcissist has made them believe that everything they have gotten they have deserved. Even though this is utterly untrue, it is hard to make someone who has suffered from narcissistic abuse realize that none of it is their fault. At the end of the day, pretty much anyone can become the target of a narcissist. The most important thing that you can do is to pay attention to the new partners you are bringing into your life to make sure it does not end with the abuse and toxicity that comes along with a narcissist.

# Chapter 5

## A Healthy Date vs. a Date With a Narcissist & Other Clues to Help You Decide If You Are Dating a Narcissist

Most people have been on a date or two in their life, if not many more. Some of those dates may have been excellent, while others were in the record books for being the worst. If you have been on many dates, it is likely that you have been on a date with a narcissist; however, you may not have even realized it. That's part of the problem, and most people don't realize they're dealing with a narcissist until it's too late.

In this chapter, we're going to discuss what a healthy date looks like compared to a date with a narcissist. Getting yourself prepared can also help to keep you protected. There are some very clear signs that may seem confusing.

Once you have worked your way through this chapter, your confusion will become clearer. You may even realize that you have met several narcissists in the past.

We will also provide you with information on how to determine if you are actually dating a narcissist or not. Alongside of the traits that we laid out in the previous chapter, there are also some tendencies that the narcissist has. Pairing these two pieces of information can give you exactly what you need to determine whether or not your current partner is a toxic narcissist or somebody worth keeping around.

Whether you have been abused by a narcissist or you're simply trying to learn more about it to keep yourself protected, learning about what a date with a narcissist looks like can be truly advantageous. Narcissists work in specific patterns and behaviors. You simply need to watch out for the signals. Let's take a look at a few different scenarios that can help you peg whether or not you are currently dating a narcissist or not.

You must understand that under narcissistic personality disorder, there are a few different subtypes. These are the malignant, closet, and exhibitionist groups. While each group has similarities when it comes to personality, they are also quite different.

The most common and recognizable subtype is the exhibitionist group.

When people are asking whether or not there is a way to spot a narcissist quickly, they're typically asking about the narcissist that is an exhibitionist, and that is what we are going to look at today when discussing healthy dates versus dates with narcissists.

As it has been discussed, the narcissist is fantastic at exaggeration. They do not see their flaws and will make their good qualities seem better than everyone else is. If you don't admire them, there is going to be a problem. Everything they do, say, or have is the best, and they will disregard what you have to say because, to them, it is simply untrue. Your opinion and voice don't even register.

Recognizing this type of behavior on a date isn't as hard as one may think. Take a moment and think about the last few times you have been on a date, did they ask you your opinion about where you wanted to eat? Was any consideration made into your different likes or dislikes when it comes to the type of restaurant you like to go to? Does your prospective partner expect that you are going to feel his choices always best and admire him for the choices he makes?Each of these questions is pretty good clues into the kind of person that you are dealing with.

When you are not taken into consideration but expected to respond with the admiration, it is a pretty good sign that you are on an unhealthy date with a narcissist.

If you were dating someone and it was healthy, they would take your opinion into consideration. Sure, it can be fun for your partner to plan a date without asking your opinion so that it is a surprise, but it should not be every single time you go out, and if they are planning it for you, they are obviously taking you into consideration when making choices about where to go. When you are in a healthy relationship and on a healthy date, adoration will not be expected.

There are definitely some red flags that you can watch out for in terms of grandiosity. They can definitely help clue you in as to whether or not you're dating a narcissist. Let's take a look at a few items that can help indicate the trait of grandeur.

- They refer to themselves and everything in their lives as the best.

- They always know how to "perfectly" handle every situation.

- All of their achievements are exaggerated.

- They name drop.

- They always talk about themselves and rarely ask about you.

- It appears as if they are bored when you talk about yourself.

- On the rare occurrence, they do ask about you, and they quickly move the conversation back to them.

- They will only become interested after finding out you were wealthy, powerful, or famous.

- Most of the time, it seems like they are only half-listening.

After you have been hurt by a narcissist, these red flags may be extremely easy to see. Even if you have never been hurt by one, take the time to think back on previous dates that you have been on, and it is likely you can find at least one person that has many of the above-listed traits. When you can recognize what you are dealing with in the beginning, it gives you the opportunity to get out of a soon-to-be toxic situation so that you protect yourself, your sanity, and your future.

Another behavior that is usually pretty recognizable when you are on a date with a narcissist is when they start to act omnipotent.

The narcissist always believes that they are right, so this leads them to lecture people whether or not they know what they are talking about. They think that their advice is always the best advice, so they handed out freely whether people ask for it or not.

When you are on a date with someone, this type of behavior is also pretty easy to recognize. On the rare occurrence that they are listening to you about your life, they will be happy to give you advice on how to fix it without you even asking. They will continue to focus on your flaw and provide you with their thoughts, which, in their opinion, are flawless even if you try to change the subject.

In this same situation, if you disagree with what they have to say, it will be taken as an insult. The narcissist will then likely verbally attack you in some sort of way. They want to make you become defensive and force you into an argument so that they can get the high they feel when they think that they have one. You must understand that arguing with a narcissist is impossible, and you will never win. Unfortunately, the only way to sate the narcissist is for you to concede. Peace will only come when you admit you were wrong, even when it is completely untrue.

If you are early in a relationship and something like this happens, and you don't accept blame, it is very likely that you are just going to want to stand up and walk out. The narcissist is never going to let this happen. Just as you are having this thought of leaving, they will stand up, make a degrading comment, and walk away.

When you are in a relationship with someone, and you are having dates that are healthy, you will not be goaded into an argument for simply disagreeing. Your flaws or problems will not be instantly corrected with the magical words of your partner. Instead of trying to force their opinions and beliefs on you, they will help you look at different solutions. If you decide you don't want to discuss it anymore, they will happily move onto a different subject.

When you are involved in dates that are healthy, both party's opinions and ideas should matter. Nobody has the best of everything, and decent people understand that your opinions do not always need to align. Someone offering their opinion is no big deal as long as they understand that it is simply an opinion. Trying to force someone to not only take your opinion but also show you adoration over it is not a sign of a healthy relationship.

The behavior of omnipotence also comes with a variety of red flags. As noted, red flags are a great indicator of the type of person you are dealing with. You do need to make sure you spend the time to actually look for red flags and pay attention to them when you do realize that they are there. Many people will ignore red flags and gut instincts. When this happens, they typically end up in detrimental situations that can lead to total toxicity and abuse in their lives.

Here are some red flags you should definitely watch out for:

- They make statements about how they are always right.

- You hear them say others should listen to them more frequently.

- They tell you how to live your life.

- They consistently tell you that you are doing things wrong. Then they tell you what you must do, so things do not go bad.

- They love to brag about times they were proven right.

- You can see it brings them a joy to prove others wrong.

- You are expected to agree with whatever they say.

- There is nothing they don't know about.

- If challenged, they become angry or irritated.

Each one of these items is actually pretty noticeable when you are present at the moment. You may not notice it on the first date, but if you continue to date somebody, you are certainly going to be aware of their standard behavior consists of the items above. The more things they do on this list, the more likely it is that you have a narcissist on your hands, and you need to move in the other direction.

When you are on an unhealthy date with a toxic narcissist, another behavior you may notice is that they are excellent at devaluing things. Putting other people down comes easy to them, and they tend to say extremely hateful remarks about anyone or anything that they dislike. Status means everything to the narcissist, so they will frequently compare things. Doing this devalues one of the two things being compared, every time. They cannot just look at something as being good; it must always be compared to something else so that they can pinpoint what is best.

This behavior, like the ones above, is not actually very hard to recognize if you know what you are looking for. If your date asks you a question about a choice you've made, and it does not line up with the choice that they would make, they're going to show you exactly why you were wrong. The lecture will not be kind or compassionate.

You will be expected to immediately change your opinion, and if you don't, a negative outburst is certainly going to occur.

Another good example of this would be extremely negative comments about the people that are around you. If you have noticed that your date makes ugly comments that are so appalling, you figure they must be joking. It is not a good sign. Narcissists can be extremely judgmental, and it will definitely be shown with their words. Cutting people down for the smallest things or for having differing opinions is certainly something you are going to come into contact with when dealing with a narcissist.

When you are on a healthy date, it is unlikely that you will hear your partner say anything negative about anyone, unless something truly awful happens. People tend to try and be polite to those around them, and this is especially true in public. Additionally, you will probably never hear the kind of abhorrent things come out of the mouth of a non-narcissist that you will a narcissist. They have no sense of care when it comes to other people who, in turn, allows them to say things that most people would not be ok with saying.

As with the above behaviors, there are definitely red flags that can show you if devaluing is part of the personality of the person you are on a date with.

Let's take a moment and look at some of the signs that you may see if devaluing is going to be something you will face:

- They only say hateful things about their ex-partners.

- They are insulted quickly and easily.

- When insulted, they retaliate.

- They consistently make negative comments about others.

- There is no pleasing them.

- They enter into arguments or debates easily.

- They have many people that they refer to as "enemies."

- They can't let things go.

- You find yourself questioning if they are joking due to the abhorrent things that they say.

If you notice that your date is treating other people this way, you must realize that at one point or another, they are going to be treating you with way. It may take a while, but at the end of the day, you are only an object to the narcissist, and criticizing you is a great way to keep you under their thumb.

# Other Clues You Might Be Dating a Narcissist

We have tried to give you a lot of insight to help you decide whether or not you have started dating a narcissist. Here we're going to provide you with a few more clues if you're still unable to figure it out. The more you learn, the easier it is going to be to truly understand what you are up against if you are, indeed, entering into a relationship with a narcissist.

We all have moments in life where we act selfishly. It is a completely normal thing for people to do, but the narcissist will take selfishness to a whole new level. They tend to not even try to hide the fact that they believe their needs are the most important thing and that they must be met. The selfish behaviors of the narcissist start to show themselves relatively quickly. If you notice that your partner not only puts themselves ahead of you but also expects you to do the same, it is a pretty good warning sign of narcissism.

If you have ever been in an argument with a narcissist, you will easily understand that there is literally no way that you can win. In the narcissist's eyes, they are never wrong, which means, in turn, if you disagree with them, you are inevitably wrong. They will act out in a variety of ways.

They may simply start by stating you are wrong and then giving you the silent treatment. If you continue to try and make your point, it is likely, and they will get angry. In extreme cases, they may even turn violent.

Narcissists are also infamous for convincing people that they are the dramatic ones. They will try and make their partner feel as if every fight is their fault. They will twist your words and your actions so that they can make you feel guilty when realistically, you have nothing to feel bad or guilty about. Anytime you try to bring up an issue that is bothering you, and it is likely that they will tell you that you are blowing it out of proportion. Additionally, they will probably try to make you feel crazy for simply trying to show them your perspective. If you continue to resist them, it is likely to end in another argument.

Extreme mood swings are also very common when you are dealing with a narcissist. They do this on purpose to try and keep their victims confused. They feel that this confusion provides them with more power and control over the person and the relationship. One moment they will be showering you with love and affection, and the next minute you will be treated as if you are the lowest specimen on earth. Just as you start to feel rejected and as if maybe it is time to leave, they will switch the roll again just to draw you back in.

The behavior of a narcissist is absolutely exhausting. Most people, at one point or another, will start to pull away from the narcissist that is controlling their life. If the narcissist notices that you are withdrawing from him, it is extremely likely that they are going to get angry. They may decide to flirt with other people in front of you or even go to the length of cheating to try and cause jealousy. If they are truly concerned that they are losing you, it is likely that they will threaten to leave first, as this plays better with their false ego.

When you are in a healthy relationship and dating someone, they should make you feel better about yourself. In the beginning, the narcissist may build you up some, but that is not going to last very long. If you are dating a narcissist, it is likely that you feel worse about yourself then you have in a long time, if ever. With repeated criticisms, gaslighting tactics, and the inability to take any blame, the narcissist will slowly but surely beat down your sense of self.

If you have been dating a narcissist for a while, you may notice that depending on where you are and who is around, they act like a completely different person. While around other people or in crowds, they will turn on the charm. Their charisma is unparalleled, and people are simply drawn to them. Once you are back behind closed doors, you will not be dealing with the same person.

They will lose control over their emotions quickly. This is especially true if they feel that you are not providing them with the attention admiration that they feel they deserve. If you ever feel like you are dealing with someone who has a split personality, depending on the situation, you are likely dealing with a narcissist.

# Chapter 6

# How the Narcissist Reels You Back In & Tips and Tricks to Keep You Safe While Dating a Narcissist

When you are in a relationship with a narcissist, getting out of it can be very difficult. Even if the narcissist is the one that ends it, it does not necessarily mean that it is over. The narcissist loves to play games. Just because the relationship has ended does not mean that they are done playing games with you.

In this chapter, we are going to look at the tactics a narcissist uses to reel you back in. Depending on the situation, it can obviously look very different. When you are ready for the games, they are going to try and play it can make it easier to refuse to participate. When you deny a narcissist attention, you have a better chance that they are going to leave you alone.

If the relationship you are in is with a narcissist and you have not decided to leave yet, you could be putting yourself in danger. In this chapter, we are also going to include some different tips and tricks that you can deploy to keep yourself safe. Some of them may work better than others. This will depend on the specific narcissist that you are dealing with. As we know, narcissists have similar traits, but at the end of the day, we are all individuals, so there will absolutely be differences as well.

## How the Narcissist Reels You Back In

If you have stepped away from the narcissist in your life, it is likely that they are going to go to great lengths to reaffirm their hold on you. Due to the fact that they will go to such lengths to get you back, it may make you believe that they are actually remorseful for the things that they have done. This is never the case when you are dealing with a narcissist.

In all reality, they are making a calculated move. They will do their best to catch you in a moment of weakness so that they can play on your sentimentality. You need to be especially careful if you know that you are feeling vulnerable or you are in a state of reflection.

These give the narcissist a great opening to set the bait and then lure you in. The narcissist loves to play with your emotions. Their hope is to soften you up to the point of reconciliation.

Many narcissists will use the hoovering technique. It is exceptionally manipulative and works beautifully to suck the victim of the narcissist back in. When narcissists use the hoovering technique, they will show you how they have changed. They may even admit fault in some of their actions. It is important to note that no part of the narcissist actually believes that they did something wrong; they are simply playing a game and are willing to lie and deceive to get you back.

They refer to this tactic as hoovering because, like a vacuum cleaner, they are trying to suck you in just to continue to treat you like dirt. They want to keep picking you up and knocking you over so they can continue to feel superior. They need power and control over you and will get it by any means necessary. The narcissist may go a long period of time before you hear from them again, but eventually, it is going to happen.

While using this tactic, the narcissist is going to try and trick you verbally.

Not only will they try to use their words, but they will also use their behaviors to try and lure you back into their narcissistic trap. Things they say and do are extremely effective at getting people back into their grips so that they can continue controlling and abusing you. Let's take a look at some of the different things the narcissist may say and do while hoovering you.

When you are with a narcissist, you've probably experienced them disappearing, giving you the silent treatment, and in general, going back and forth. At one point or another, you may have even told them that you can't do it anymore and told them that the relationship needed to end. When using the hoovering tactic, the narcissist will come back insincerely tell you that they have been thinking about what you said, and their only desire is to make things work between the two of you. After making this statement, it is also very likely that they tell you they have decided to seek out a counselor to help them handle their problems.

Many people, when they hear this, will jump right back into a relationship because they think a person genuinely is trying to get better and that the relationship can heal. In reality, this is a trick that is favorited by the narcissist. They're simply trying to buy time, and even if they do seek out a therapist, they will not be honest with them.

It is very likely while seeing a therapist that the narcissist is going to try to twist things so that it looks like you are the bad guy. They may even pick up some of the language used around their therapist's office to continue and try to make you feel as if you are the one causing the problems.

This tactic works so well because when you truly love someone, regardless of if they are narcissist or not, you want to believe that they are sincere, and you can get back to feeling like you did at the beginning of your relationship with them. The narcissist will do a variety of things in combination with saying they're seeing a therapist to help your relationship move forward, such as crying, and the tactic works extremely well. However, before you know it, life will be right back to the same mess that it was before you decided to leave them, and realistically, the abuse tends to get significantly worse.

While this tactic is used frequently, it would be very difficult to find a narcissist that actually saw problems with themselves and tried to change for their relationship. It really is just a mind game, and it will likely end up in their victim needing to see a counselor to start trying to undo the damage that is continuously being done.

Dealing with a narcissist is understanding that they do not feel there is anything about them that needs to change, so there are simple statements of I need to see therapy so that things with me become better is extreme trickery.

If you have been through more than one break up with a narcissist, it is likely they are going to try and use another person against you. They will try and tell you they met somebody while you were broken up but that they mean nothing to them. They will say that they were only with this other person because they felt as if you could not totally invest yourself in them. In reality, they will say these kinds of things so that you will disregard their infidelity and come back to them.

This tactic will hurt the victim's self-esteem and give the narcissist an ego boost as it will make it look as if they are sought after by many different people. It is also a great chance for them to use techniques like gaslighting against you. The theory behind them doing this is that they can get you to become afraid of losing them completely, and this is a great motivation for you to stick around and try and keep their attention.

When this is occurring, many people do not realize it is a simple pattern like most things in regard to a narcissist.

It may be hard to accept that they have likely been cheating on you for quite some time, not just when you were broken up, but it is probably the truth. Lies and deceit come very easy to the narcissist, and their only intention is to win the game; it's just unfortunate that the game involves you.

Another thing that the narcissist likes to try and do too lure you back in is to ask if you can just be friends. If they have been unfaithful, which led to a breakup, you probably heard all of the shortcomings, and they could think of about you to concrete the fact that you are not their ideal partner. After this, eventually, they will come back talking about how they met their mistake and stating that they can't see their life without you. They will make it look like they don't care if you are simply friends or more than friends; they just want you around. In all reality, the narcissist will never want to just be your friend, and they will want to take it to another level.

If you do decide to try and just be their friend, you need to be prepared for what you are about to ensue. They will continually try to be intimate with you, but because you aren't together, they will also continue to be intimate with other people. The narcissist doesn't want anyone else to have a chance of being with you and will do everything in their power to make sure that you stick by their side and that they can continue with their nefarious games.

Sometimes, they will use phrases like you simply aren't the right fit for me. As the victim, you have likely absorbed a lot of emotional outbursts from the narcissist and done your best to straighten things out and fix the relationship. This is fruitless, and eventually, the narcissist will seemingly end things. In reality, this ploy is not used to actually get rid of you; it is used to try and get you to win them back. This provides the narcissist with the needed supply of attention that they seek as you try to resuscitate the relationship and prove to them that you are the right person to be in their lives.

There are also times they will try and lure you back into their tangled web by apologizing for hurting you and stating that they will find a way to make it up. Every subtype of a narcissist is known for using this tactic due to the fact that the people they target are typically empathetic, tolerant, cooperative, and forgiving. Narcissists know this and will exploit it as much as possible. They understand when they approach you with gifts and emotional outreaching that you are likely to turn to them with forgiveness and compassion. As the victim, you may be able to see a future where things are wonderful between the two of you, and the narcissist knows this, using it to their advantage.

When it comes to reconciliation, your thoughts as compared to the narcissist's thoughts are completely different.

They will be focused on how to lure you back in and find the supply they need, all while demanding respect, loyalty, and admiration from you. There is no point in time that they're focused on having a healthy relationship and a future with you; it is always going to be about them.

Anyone that has had experience with a narcissist knows that faithfulness is not something they are known for. Often times, they will do what they can to make it look as if they have no control over their sexual misdeeds. They will frequently state that you are the only one that they truly love even though they show you otherwise on a consistent basis. You may start to feel as if these things are true as they push the fact that you're the only one that accepts them for who they are. It's funny though, as they talk about how you are the only one for them, they will also throw little digs in there to help remove even more of yourself worth.

Narcissists are great at making excuses. Not only will they state that they only love you, but they will ask questions like, isn't it your bed they always sleep in and aren't you the person that they always end up coming back to. In reality, these are just persuasive arguments used to keep you in their grips.

hey will tell you that they feel that you are unique and special, but they never actually believe those things or appreciate what it is about you that is truly special and unique. They only care that you continue to desire and admire them.

The narcissist in your life may also try and claim that they have had an epiphany. That all of a sudden, they have a true understanding that the two of you were meant to be one. They'll exclaim that they weren't able to see it before, but it is all clear to them now. You may even find that they go to great extremes and state that you should be married so that your commitment can last forever.

Unfortunately, regardless of how much you share your pain with them, the narcissist is never going to have an epiphany that makes them realize the truth of the situation. They will look as if they care and as if the things they have done, they are remorseful for, but this is never going to be the truth. This is a simple tactic to draw you in and make sure that you will give them the supply they need forever, if at all possible.

At the end of the day, the narcissist is to do everything they can to get their fix of attention and adoration. As much as you may want to believe that things could be different, you have to accept that they are never going to be.

The narcissist doesn't take morals and values into consideration because you are an object to be had in their eyes, not a human being.

With a narcissist in your life, you will never be in control of anything. Everything you do will be with a price tag attached to it, and you may end up paying with your grip on reality, your sense of self, and any self-worth you may have left. If you have broken up with a narcissist or they have left you, you must not let them back in. Everything that the narcissist says and does has been planned out, and there is the motive behind it. You will not have genuine interactions with a narcissist no matter how convincing they are, and it is always manipulation.

You should always try and remember that words come exceptionally easily to the narcissist. It is a craft that they have mastered. If any part of you can recognize the words and actions being used against you, don't disregard them. Pay attention and remove yourself from the narcissist's life before they are able to abuse you and convince you that it is your fault.

# Chapter 7

# Healing After Dating a Narcissist

Healing after you have dated a narcissist can be a very difficult thing to do. Depending on the length of the relationship will depend on how difficult it is going to be to move on. Obviously, the longer you have been abused by a narcissist, the more impact it is going to have on you as a whole. No matter how long you have been with the narcissist, once you have gotten away, you can become a whole person again.

Once you are free from the narcissist, one of the first things you should do is focus on yourself. There are many lessons to be learned after being involved with a narcissist and spending some time looking at them can make it easier to let go of the past and move on with your life. Additionally, if you take the time to look at the lessons, this has taught you it can help ensure that you do not get yourself back into the same situation.

What each and every victim of narcissistic abuse needs to understand is that while it may look like the narcissist is self-confident, they actually have no self-esteem at all. Somewhere deep down inside, they think that they are the worst people on earth. They do the things they do to try and make themselves feel better. When you start to understand this, it can help recovery to move along more quickly.

After separating yourself from a narcissist, you need to accept the situation for what it was. There may have been things about you that drew the narcissist in and areas of your character that you need to work on, but you are not the reason that everything went awry. The narcissist likely did a good job of encouraging you to blame yourself and criticize yourself, but it is time for that to end. When you can accept the fact that you are in a relationship with a narcissist, you will also be able to accept that nothing that happened was your fault, they have a personality disorder.

Focusing on yourself can help build your self-esteem and the confidence that you have in your decision making and in yourself. You are less likely to be chosen as a partner by the narcissist if you have a high level of self-esteem and self-worth. The narcissist wants to take control so that they can feel powerful.

The narcissist will not pick people with high self-confidence because they understand that once in a relationship with them, the self-confident person will easily see the emotional abuse that the narcissist is trying to cause them. From there, they will quickly move away from the toxic relationship before it can ever gain any footing.

Self-confidence allows people to recognize and accept when something simply isn't right between themselves and another person. They are able to accept that the match is no good and move on. They will stand up for themselves and refuse to take the blame that is not actually there's. Higher levels of self-esteem and confidence also allow people to understand when they're not happy and figure out the changes they need to make to regain their happiness.

So, as you can see, working on yourself and building up your confidence and self-esteem can ensure that you are not the target of a narcissist. You will be too much of a challenge for them, and they need instant gratification. After separating yourself from a narcissist, some of the most important steps forward you can take will be to work on yourself and to start to reconnect with your thoughts, feelings, and emotions. Additionally, spending the time to work through your belief system, including your morals and your values, can improve your confidence levels even more.

Another thing you can do to make sure that you are on the correct path toward healing and that you are less likely to become the target of a narcissist is to stop judging yourself. When people doubt themselves, they become an easy target. The narcissist thrives on people that have a lot of self-doubts and know how to be appealing to them from the very beginning. With their superficial strength and confidence, they try to charm you. Their attention and your own self-doubt can be blinding, stopping you from seeing what is actually happening in front of you. Narcissists show their victims quickly that they believe they are weak and worthless.

While the things that transpired may not have been your fault, you do need to take accountability for the fact that you did choose to be with this person. Narcissists obviously use lies and manipulation that make them seem irresistible. They are charming and create a persona that just about anyone could fall for. However, there were likely times you should have went with your gut instinct or that you ignored red flags, and those are things that need to be accepted and that you need to take responsibility for.

Learning how to believe in yourself does not happen overnight, but it is definitely something that you should work on. Many people like to use daily affirmations to help them remember what it is about themselves that is great.

Working on getting physically healthy can also help with your mental health status. Not only that, but eating right and simply trying to take care of yourself on a daily basis can really have a positive impact on the way that you see yourself and how much you are able to believe in yourself. Once you start to see yourself in a more positive light, narcissists will be less attracted to you.

As you are healing and working on yourself, you should take a moment to look at your own level of co-dependency and issues that you may have with your ego. Looking into these two things can give you a better understanding of why you went to such great lengths to protect somebody that was abusing you. This opportunity can allow you to become kinder and more compassionate with yourself. Additionally, it will connect your mind, body, and spirit together so that you become a whole person.

Grounding yourself is also extremely important when you are healing from narcissistic abuse. They live in a land of fantasy, and it is likely that you have been drawn into this world. Your thought patterns may not be completely rational, and your sense of reality is very likely to be skewed from the experience that you have had with the narcissist.

You need to make sure you are looking at how things actually are rather than how they could be or how you perceived them to be while you were in the throes of chaos that the narcissist creates.

When you are in a relationship that is abusive, it can be extremely powerful, and it can warp your sense of self and your sense of reality in tragic ways. Work with the people that you trust the most to help find balance and reenter yourself in reality. This can make moving past the issues that the narcissist causes easier and allow you to be present in the moment and move through the pain and chaos that you experienced.

It is unfortunate that we have to suggest this; however, when you are trying to emotionally heal from dating a narcissist, you need to remove all contact that you have with them. You should have an understanding at this point that they will do anything to suck you back into their world of chaos. If you truly wish to heal and move on, you must not allow this to happen. There is nothing wrong with changing your phone number, email address, and blocking them from accessing you on social media. All you are doing is protecting yourself and that is exactly the correct course of action.

When you are recovering from narcissistic abuse, you need to be extremely patient and kind to yourself. You will have not received any patience or kindness for the duration of your relationship with a narcissist, so this may seem difficult to do. You need to understand that you have been through a traumatic situation, and it is going to take time until the effects are reversed. Being kind to yourself is equally as important as it will help to rebuild your self-esteem and ground you in exactly who you are and what you are genuinely worth.

With all of the manipulation and gaslighting that happens in a narcissistic relationship, it is very likely that you no longer participate in activities that used to bring you joy. Additionally, you may have distanced yourself from people that you enjoy being around. Once you are set free from the narcissistic relationship, it is important on your path to healing to rediscover the activities and people that bring you happiness.

When you start to feel passionate about the things that used to be very fulfilling to you, it helps set you in the right direction. You will more easily be able to see your true path, and it will help you rebuild your confidence level. Trying new and different activities can also be beneficial as they can help you focus on yourself rather than the past.

When your life starts to calm down because you are no longer dealing with a narcissist on a daily basis, it can actually be a little scary. Things in your life have been in a state of chaos for the entire amount of time you are with the narcissist, and it will take a little bit for you to adjust to the calmness of your new life as it is unfamiliar. It is absolutely OK to take time to adjust to this. Know that it is a transitional period and what eventually the normalcy will be a great relief as it will no longer feel unfamiliar.

Some people get very upset with themselves when they start to grieve about their past narcissistic relationship. You should not feel ashamed if you are grieving what you have left behind. You have suffered a loss in a variety of ways, and grieving is a normal part of the process. It is, however, important that you remember things are going to get better, and you will feel happier than you have in a long time as long as you move forward with kindness, understanding, and compassion toward not only yourself but to others as well.

When you are on the path to healing, moving forward is important even if it is in the smallest steps. You need to remember that what you are working on is finding the true reality and a genuine sense of who you are as these things are frequently lost after being in a relationship with a narcissist.

While it is important to spend time working through the past, you should not spend too much time there. When we are completely focused on the past, we are not allowing ourselves to move on or be present in the wonderful experiences that could be happening right in front of us. Be mindful of the release and relief that you feel now that you are on the outside of the narcissistic relationship that was tearing you down and be appreciative of the future that you are going to be able to build now that you are away from it.

Oftentimes people forget that there are many others in the same situation. Unfortunately, there are a large number of narcissists in the world, and they are great at drawing people to them just so that they can cause destruction in their lives. Remembering that you are not alone and that there are many people going through what you are going through can help give you the courage and strength to face what is happened to you and allow yourself to move past it.

If you have been in a relationship with a narcissist for a decent length of time, you may have quite a lot of work to do in the realm of healing. Know that you do not need to take this burden on by yourself. As previously mentioned, surrounding yourself with friends and family members that will help support you through this difficult time is extremely advantageous.

In addition, reaching out to a therapist that is well versed in narcissistic personality disorder can be extremely beneficial. There is absolutely nothing wrong with reaching out for help.

Therapists that specialize in personality disorders can be extremely helpful in allowing you to learn how to cope with the experience you have had. They can also give you insight into different areas that you may need to work on so that you do not become a target of someone who is a narcissist. They will be able to provide you with the understanding and the tools you need to truly heal and move on with your life so that you can live the best version of it.

When you need support, another great idea is to look for different groups that offer support for those that have suffered from abuse or specifically narcissistic abuse. You will probably be surprised at how many options are available for you in terms of support groups that can help with your recovery. These support groups meet in physical form, and they can also be found on the Internet. Online support groups offer easy access to people that will understand exactly what you are trying to process and move through. It may seem intimidating to reach out at first but find your bravery and give it a try. The results are sure to be helpful.

After suffering narcissistic abuse, it is going to be very hard for you to put trust in other people. Allowing yourself to be vulnerable will feel like it is impossible. When you start down the path toward healing, you will need to work on learning how to trust people, including yourself, again. The only true way to start trusting other people is to really get to know yourself. Additionally, you need to learn how to have faith in yourself to be able to have faith in others. Be open to learning your own personal truths so that you can be open to letting other people in.

As you are working on connecting with yourself, you also really need to connect with your inner voice. Intuition plays a major role in helping us protect ourselves against situations and people that will end up being toxic. Many of us ignore this inner voice by rationalizing what is occurring. You are doing an injustice to yourself when you start to justify the bad behaviors of the people that you allow into your life.

Connecting with your inner voice is not as difficult as it may seem. Many people find it easy to connect with themselves when they start to practice things like guided breathing exercises, meditation, and yoga. There are also a lot of self-help materials that can guide you in the right direction when searching for a true connection between your physical self and your inner self.

Use the strength of your inner voice to your advantage by learning how to listen to it instead of rationalizing it away.

Many people also find it to be extremely healing to write their experiences down. Externalizing the mess that the narcissist has made inside, you can be extremely cathartic. If writing isn't your thing, you can also externalize your experience with things like dancing, massages, or even simple conversations with friends. They can help you let go of the chaos and confusion that comes every time you think about your situation with a narcissist.

You should also take the time to inquire about yourself. While you are working through the difficulties you have faced, you can actually find a lot of growth and enlightenment. When you can figure out what your biggest vulnerabilities are, you can then work toward alleviating yourself of them or at minimum protecting those pieces.

When you start looking at yourself on a deeper level, you may find that you have a need for security. Perhaps your father was a bit neglectful, or he was absent in life. You may find that traumas from childhood are the reason you keep being lured in by the narcissist. We all want a sense of security and narcissists are great at acting like they can provide that.

What we all need to realize is that we provide our own security. It is not found in other people.

Others will find when they look at that deeper level that they have a need for adoration or acknowledgment. What you must understand is that the narcissist sees these things extremely easy and will take advantage of them as quickly as possible. Instead of searching for these things from other people, you need to find them within yourself. We're not saying this is going to be an easy task; however, it is definitely a challenge worth facing. Talking to yourself in a positive way can help you learn how to acknowledge when you have done something good. Additionally, learning how to nurture yourself on every level is also extremely important. Your mind, body, and soul all need attention from you, not from other people.

Oftentimes when we are trying to heal, it is important that we take time to look at our childhood. Trying to create cohesion within oneself can be difficult, and if you want lasting results, then reviewing your history is important. You need to eliminate any pain that is lingering and allow yourself to let go of the people or situations that caused you this pain.

There is a child inside each and every one of us. Allow yourself to hear them, see them, and provide them with the love and understanding that they need so that you can guide yourself toward living your best life. It can be hard to look past trauma in the face, but at the end of the day, it will be extremely cathartic and freeing. When you let go of the burdens that have been weighing you down for so long, you will be more equipped to love yourself and stand up for the person that you are when somebody is trying to tear you down.

You should also take the time to learn about healthy relationships versus narcissistic relationships. This book has given you a great look at what it is like to date a narcissist, but if this is some of the most prevalent experiences in your life, you may not completely understand what it is to have a healthy relationship. Gaining an understanding as to what a healthy relationship actually is can help ensure that you do not allow toxicity to seep into your life again.

When you are in a healthy relationship, you will be able to honestly communicate with your partner and know that they are listening and trying to understand your perspective. They will not only be concerned about themselves, but they will also be concerned about you and how you are doing. You will feel safe to open up to them without being worried about what type of retaliation may happen with your expressions.

When you first start to try and enter into a healthy relationship, it can be very confusing. Healthy relationships don't look anything like the relationships you have had with narcissists, and this can leave an unsettling feeling of disbelief. Learning how to trust that there are actually people in the world that I care about others and can be compassionate and kind is a hard pill to swallow while you are working through healing from narcissistic abuse.

While you should always take your time getting to know someone if they continuously show you that they are reliable and supportive, eventually you will start to believe it. Continue to be honest with yourself so that you can be honest with others, and finding someone who is truly going to treat you the way that you deserve to be treated is just around the corner.

When you take the time to truly heal from the abuse that you have suffered from a narcissist, it will make you a better-rounded person. You will be more integrated into your life, and you will feel more whole than you ever have before. It is likely that you will be more mindful and aware of not only yourself but those that are around you. In addition, your level of self-love will grow so that eventually, you can share it with the world around you.

While no one should have to suffer at the hands of a narcissist, it is, unfortunately, something that happens on a daily basis. Once you have gotten away from the toxic situation, you need to look at it as an opportunity to truly grow. You will have to face a variety of difficult things in regard to yourself and the relationships in your life. With personal kindness and compassion, you will be able to lift yourself up out of the dark and start to truly enjoy becoming your best self.

# Chapter 8

# Spotting a Narcissist on the First Date

When you can recognize a narcissist on the first date, it makes it very easy to walk away before any harm could possibly come to you. As previously mentioned, there are different types of narcissists, so learning their methods on a first date is the only way to truly keep yourself protected. In this chapter, we're going to take a look at the different types of narcissists and how you can expect them to act on a first date so that you can get away from them quickly before they are able to pull you into their tangled web.

The titles of the subtypes of narcissists vary depending on who you talk to. We are going to look at the exhibitionist, toxic, and closet narcissist. You should also understand that depending on who or what you are referencing, there may be different amounts of subtypes when it comes to narcissism.

Covert narcissists are also referred to as closet narcissists, whereas toxic narcissists can also be referred to as malignant narcissists. No matter the name you put on them the information you gain about each category is what actually matters.

If you are dealing with an exhibitionist narcissist, you will be dealing with someone that has a great need for attention and admiration. We have discussed a lot about the exhibitionist narcissist in this book. The closet narcissist wants to be associated with someone of power or someone that they admire. Toxic narcissists have a need to dominate others and make them feel completely worthless and useless. There are similarities and differences between each of the subtypes of narcissism.

It is important to know and recognize each narcissistic subgroup so that you can understand exactly what you are dealing with. It can also provide you with the information you need to understand the effects of the relationship. Recognizing narcissistic traits like a lack of empathy, anger, being extremely conscious of status and being extremely sensitive to criticism are all traits that every narcissist will have.

Each of the narcissistic subtypes has a pattern when it comes to relationships.

More often than not, the exhibitionist narcissist is who is focused on, which can make identifying the other types a bit more difficult. Most people will have a much harder time realizing that they are with a narcissist if they are not an exhibitionist narcissist.

You may go for a long period of time without seeing narcissistic traits in your partner and wonder if their narcissism is something that suddenly came to fruition. The easy answer is no. A narcissistic personality disorder, when we are children, even though it's not going to be diagnosable until we are adults. You simply did not recognize the traits to begin with.

When narcissism becomes more obvious, it is usually because something has threatened the narcissist's ego. The narcissist's defenses will rise, and it will make them act out with the common traits that we see among narcissists. This acting out makes their behaviors much more noticeable which is why you have suddenly been able to recognize the fact that you are in a relationship with someone who struggles with narcissism. Even if you hadn't seen them in the beginning, once you notice it, it will be hard to push their behaviors to the wayside.

If you start to look at the time you have spent together, it will become easier to pinpoint their behavioral issues and you will start to understand that their narcissism has had a negative effect on your relationship from the beginning.

Now we're going to specifically look at the subtypes listed above and how they are going to act when you are on a first date with them. 1st dates give a great amount of information as to how life may be if you continue on in a relationship with a person. You do have to remember that on the first date people will always put their best self in front of you. However, if their best self is still putting you off, it is a good clue that you're not going to enjoy being around them if you progress into a relationship with them.

For the most part, narcissists usually give themselves up pretty quickly. They don't always understand how loudly their actions speak. They have patterns in their relationships that are repeated time and time again. So, you need to be observant when you first start to meet people so that you can understand what their true colors are and what a future with them may look like.

# Exhibitionist or Overt Narcissists

When most people think of the term narcissist, this is the narcissist that they are thinking about. They need to be the center of attention at all moments and will do just about anything to ensure that they are. They have an insane sense of entitlement and believe that they deserve special treatment. The exhibitionist narcissist will dominate conversations, and they are extremely confident.

If the exhibitionist narcissist is feeling insecure about the situation, they will use the tactics of grandiose, omnipotent, and devaluing defenses. They hide behind these defenses so that others will not see how much they doubt themselves. There is an inability to present themselves in a normal way. The narcissist will require that you see how special and perfect they are. They hold themselves in such high regard that they will also expect that others will believe their point of view without thought. To the exhibitionist narcissist, all other people are below them.

The exhibitionist narcissist facade of being above everyone else is rather thin, which also means it can be disrupted quite easily.

Due to this fact they will be extremely sensitive to anything that makes them feel slighted. When you are dealing with an exhibitionist narcissist, they're going to get angry quickly and will cause arguments over the smallest things. They are also quick to cruelty due to their extreme lack of empathy.

When you are on a first date with an exhibitionist narcissist, they are going to brag about their accomplishments as much as you would possibly let them. Not only will they draw attention to their accomplishments even if they are minor, but they will also continuously tell you stories where they played the part of the hero. While they are making themselves look heroic, they will also be doing a great job of devaluing others. They tend to be very condescending and cruel when it comes to telling stories where somebody protested against the narcissist's thoughts or actions.

As they are doing this, it is likely that your reactions to the way they are acting are not so good, but the narcissist will never notice. They are under the true belief that everyone will agree with them because, at the end of the day, they are right. So, regardless of how you react to the narcissist, they will disregard that and continue on with the stories and achievements of their lives that they think are impressing you and swaying you to their side.

The exhibitionist narcissist is bossy and extremely insensitive. Their expectation is that you are going to agree with everything they have to say and admire them for it. If you disagree with them, they will take it as criticism even if that is not the case, and they will meet you with devaluation. Remember, they are in constant need of the reassurance that they are perfect, special, uncommon, and always correct.

## The Closet or Covert Narcissist

When you are dealing with a closet narcissist, you are dealing with something completely different than an exhibitionist narcissist. They greatly prefer when the spotlight is not on them as it makes them uncomfortable. They have a longing to be considered special, but they're also extremely conflicted about it. More often than not, they believe that they will be attacked if they seek out admiration in a flashy way and this typically comes from their childhood.

The closet narcissist probably had a parent who was an exhibitionist narcissist that completely devalued them. They were likely only rewarded when they were providing their exhibitionist narcissist parents with admiration and attention.

This oftentimes causes the grandiosity of the narcissist to be buried deeply. The insecurities of the closet narcissist are much greater than the exhibitionist narcissist, and it shows in their demeanor.

They will not allow themselves to be the center of attention because they feel as if it exposes them and their vulnerabilities too much. Because they were attacked and devalued as children, they are oftentimes afraid of allowing people to see that they are flawed. The closet narcissist will find ways of attaching themselves to others and getting others to attach themselves to them. The things they will attach themselves to are typically items they admire or feel are special. This will allow them to feel special by simply being associated with the person or item.

The closet narcissist is not going to be demanding in a full-frontal sort of way; however, they will still manipulate situations so that the outcome is what they want. They are excellent at playing the victim so that you will take pity on them. This opens the door for them to be able to persuade you to meet their wants and desires. This type of narcissist is excellent at playing nice, even when they feel completely different inside.

Those that fall into the category of a closet narcissist allow confident people to use them. They get their high from the praise received by being associated with people or things that they admire. They idealize situations and people, all while striving to receive appreciation and attention.

If a closet narcissist picks you to be with it is because they are idealizing you and seeing you as perfect, unique, and special. Whatever it is that they find special about you, they have full belief that your glory is their glory and that your uniqueness will rub off on them. The small amounts of approval that they are given they hold on to extremely tightly. An interesting fact is that the closet narcissist will often end up in a relationship with an exhibitionist narcissist. This occurs due to the fact that they feel they can feed off of the grandiosity of the exhibitionist narcissist.

Being in a relationship with a closet narcissist may not be as abusive as being in a relationship with the other types, but it is still not an ideal situation. You will absolutely be dealing with someone who has a personality disorder, which means they will never be able to be fully invested in a healthy and meaningful relationship. They will still lie and manipulate you to try and make themselves feel better about who they are. Recognizing the closet narcissist is probably the hardest subtype to recognize.

# Toxic Narcissists

Toxic narcissists are extremely difficult to deal with. They not only need to be the center of attention, but they also want to completely dominate other people. The toxic narcissist tends to be more sadistic and find joy in causing other people pain. They're focused on people obeying them and fearing them. This is very similar to an exhibitionist narcissist, but the level is even more extreme.

The toxic narcissist may have been an exhibitionist narcissist at one point but has fallen deeper into the hole of narcissism. They will more than likely be angry and bitter at themselves and at the world. This is due to the fact that they feel they were unable to reach their unrealistic fantasies and goals.

The toxic narcissist will also have a great amount of envy toward anybody that has something that they want. They have no need to try and be constructive, and their only intent is to bring other people down. They don't care how obvious it is that they have malicious intent, and they will present it without regard. This is very much like a bully who openly terrorizes another person.

It is important to note that toxic narcissists may not be quite as overt with their actions and intentions.

They may manage to embarrass you or degrade you in a slightly more cunning way. These are the habits of the exhibitionist narcissist that is still in their system. Toxic narcissists are easier to pick out than others due to the fact that they don't usually care if you recognize them for what they are or not.

The relationship style of the toxic narcissist is very in your face. Their goal is to make sure that you understand that they're better than you. They will openly try and make you feel inferior or inadequate in just about every way possible. Putting you down is simply a way of life for the toxic narcissist.

There is absolutely no way that you are ever going to be able to please them enough to gain any sort of recognition. They will never praise you or make you feel good about yourself in any way. These narcissists are the best at completely removing a person's level of self-confidence. If you stay in a relationship with them, it is likely that you will have a total lack of self-confidence that is replaced with doubt.

When it comes to devaluing other people, every type of narcissist is going to do it. This enhances their own self-esteem while tearing yours apart. While all three categories will devalue others how often they do it and who they do it too can differ dramatically.

When dealing with an exhibitionist narcissist, you will find that they devalue people when they don't get the attention from them that they feel they deserve. They're also apt to devalue people if they feel that they're criticizing them. The only people that the exhibitionist narcissist will not devalue are the ones they consider holding a higher rank than they do, and as we know, this is very few people.

If you have a closet narcissist on your hands, they will actually devalue themselves more frequently than devaluing others. They are quick to apologize. It is very likely that they devalue a lot of people, but they simply keep it to themselves, or they do it behind their backs. While they are devaluing somebody, they will also withdraw from them. There are times that they will express their envy, but they will likely not talk poorly of people in public.

The toxic narcissist gets a thrill out of embarrassing other people. They are constantly seeking to knock people down a peg. Dragging someone down at first interaction is not an uncommon thing for the toxic narcissist. They may try and do this in a covert fashion, or they may be extremely blunt about devaluing others.

They don't need to wait for someone to not provide them with the attention and admiration that they seek before becoming negative and trying to devalue others, like the exhibitionist narcissist. They will devalue you from the very beginning.

As you can see, each category of narcissism does look a little different even though there are similarities that cross the different subtypes. At the end of the day, being with a narcissist regardless of the form they take is going to be detrimental to your health, sanity, happiness, and future. Being able to take a step back from the situation and really look at what is happening right in front of you is your best defense against getting into a serious relationship with a narcissist.

No matter the type that you are dealing with, there is definitely going to be signs and red flags that can be seen when you are mindful, present in the moment, and observant. We cannot express how important it is to take notice of red flags and to listen to your intuition if it is nagging you to get away from somebody you have just met. You may be fighting against what your heart thinks it wants, but in the long run, you will be providing yourself with protection against extreme abuse as every narcissist will end up abusing you.

You should also keep in mind that there is realistically no way to change the narcissist you can only make changes to yourself. Whether you have suffered from the abuse of a narcissist or not, learning about them is a great way to ensure you will never have to worry about it or not have to worry about it again. Recognizing narcissism in any form on the first date can be a challenge, but it is one that you should accept and work toward.

We have only provided you with a look at how you may be able to spot a narcissist on the first date so that you can shut it down quickly. We encourage you to continue your research so that you gain an even better understanding of narcissists and what it is that makes them tick. With your newfound understanding, you will be able to shut down their tactics before they are able to put you in a position that no one should have to be in. Always remember to listen to the people that you trust the most as they may be able to see a situation more clearly while standing on the outside of it.

As previously mentioned, different theories on narcissism exist, and touching base with all of them may be able to give you a well-rounded view of what you are facing. Obviously, most people understand that being in a relationship with a narcissist is not going to end well for them and so they want to avoid it.

We hope that you are better equipped to pinpoint a narcissist now that you have worked through this chapter. The next time you are on a first date, hopefully, any signs they are giving of-that could clue you into narcissism you will be able to recognize so you can keep yourself far away from the terror that the narcissist is sure to bring to your life.

# Conclusion

Thank you for making it through to the end of *Dating a Narcissist*, let's hope it was informative and able to provide you with all of the tools you need to achieve your goals whatever they may be.

The next step is to take what you have learned and put it into action. By stepping back and really observing and listening to your potential lover, you can tell a lot of things. Narcissists give themselves away in a variety of different fashions. You should be able to take what you have learned here and more easily decide if you are facing a narcissist or not.

It can be very difficult in the beginning, to have a clear understanding of if you are entering into a normal and healthy relationship or one that will turn into a toxic mess with just a little bit more time. Trust your gut. When we are in tune with ourselves and listen to what our instinct is trying to tell us, we are better protected.

Take the time to truly learn the tricks and tactics that a narcissist will use. Doing so will ensure that when red flags start to arise that you actually pay attention to them. If you have never been in a relationship with a narcissist, now is not the time to start. If you have, then hopefully, this book has helped you understand the situation more fully, so you will be better protected the next time you meet a narcissist.

Narcissists are great for reeling you back in, remember the ways you can avoid this constant yo-yo effect. There are a variety of tips and tricks that can help keep you safe if you are true, dating a narcissist. Getting to know real healthy love versus narcissistic love can also clue you in to the moves you need to make to find true happiness.

Finally, if you found this book useful in any way, a review on Amazon is always appreciated!

Lightning Source UK Ltd.
Milton Keynes UK
UKHW020231041220
374592UK00003B/401